# Journey to the Soul

## *Connecting to the Truth of*
## *Who You Are Through Journaling*

Diane Dandeneau™

*Journey to the Soul*
*Connecting to the Truth of Who You Are Through Journaling*

© 2016 by Diane Dandeneau

*To learn more about Diane's work, please contact her through her website:* www.dianedandeneau.com

Library of Congress Cataloging-in-Publication Data
Dandeneau, Diane
*Journey to the Soul* ~ *Connecting to the Truth of Who You Are Through Journaling/Diane Dandeneau*

ISBN: # 978-1-5136-0936-2 (Paperback)
ISBN: # 978-1-5136-0937-9 (eBook)

1. Self-Help, Journaling  2. Self-Help, Meditations  3. Self-Help, Spiritual

Cover Illustration by Diane Dandeneau
Special thanks to Cathy Rivers for editing and support.

Empowered Whole Being Press
www.EmpoweredWholeBeingPress.com

# Foreword

I have been honored to follow and support Diane through her awakening journey and to see her grow in her work and in her service to the world. Being an Aries 5 birth path, she's a powerful force in the world and has lived a fearless life as a painter, musician, writer, entrepreneur and sales leader; she has the depth of experience to be a masterful teacher.

This book is a courageous offering, opening a door for people to discover that we are all Divine. Diane shares her personal journey of discovering herself with a willingness to be vulnerable and honest. Her story reveals her courage and commitment to her path and to living her truth.

Diane is a powerful teacher with the wisdom to help others awaken through her extraordinary insights. She's a creative master and an alchemist of spiritual transformation. Her story is an excellent example of living a Divinely guided life.

I believe this small book can have an extraordinary impact on your life. It's an invitation to have a concrete and personal relationship with the Divine and a recipe to experience the unconditional love that we're all seeking.

~ Sue Frederick
Author of *Bridges to Heaven* and *I See Your Dream Job*.
www.suefrederick.com

I'm grateful to have Sue Frederick write the forward for this book, as without her, it and I might not have ever emerged from my closet.

This journey began in September of 2002, when I was at a point of suicidal depression, and living a life that I knew was completely disconnected from who I truly was. I began to write in my journals, pleading with God to tell me why I was here. To my wonder and surprise, God began to write to me through my hands and onto the paper. After two years of this incredible experience, I wrote the first version of this book, and began to teach others how to have their own relationship with the Divine through Journaling.

But then my life took a diversion back into the world, and I became distracted by a new relationship and work projects. I all but stopped writing with God in my journals, and gave up teaching.

Then, in 2010, I had a great job that I enjoyed, working as a sales director for a solar company. Things were going well, but I felt something nagging at me – like something was missing. About this time I happened to see an ad for a book called, I See Your Dream Job, and also saw that the author did intuitive sessions for people. I felt unusually drawn to explore this, so I decided to schedule a session.

That was when I first met Sue Frederick. She knew nothing about me, but through numerology, in which she is an expert, and her intuitive talents, she began to tell me who I am and why I am here. She began to describe my life purpose as a teacher and that it was my path to teach people how to discover who they truly are, through spirituality and creativity. I was dumbfounded. I asked her if she's been rummaging around my closets and reading my journals?!

Sue reminded me of the work I had started and put aside. She coached me on ways I could reclaim my gifts and step into the role of being this teacher, and inspired me to take a spiritual coaching class, publish my book, and honor and share the gifts I have been given.

I knew in my heart what she was saying was true, immediately took her advice, and within 6 months was teaching again. I have continued to work with Sue as a coach and mentor. I became an "I See Your Dream Job" coach, and have followed her journey as the amazing teacher she is, with her additional books, I See Your Soul Mate, Bridges to Heaven, and Your Divine Lens.

I am honored to call her my friend and now colleague. I'm finally publishing this book, and I'm so happy that Sue agreed to contribute to the forward.

~ Diane Dandeneau

# Table of Contents

# Preface

Thank you for opening this book and walking into the unknown. If you got past the cover, then you may be ready to walk into your own unknown. I appreciate and honor your courage.

My good friend, Bill Patterson, keeps challenging me on my use of the words "God, Truth, and Love". He said he removed those words from his vocabulary a long time ago because of how charged they are and how many meanings they carry. I have respectfully listened and considered his views, and yet I still feel compelled to use them. Because the meanings have changed over time for me, I feel it is very important to use these particular words. God no longer means to me, "the fire and brimstone guy with the beard doling out judgment and damnation". I now know "God" to be the One, the All, and Myself. I now know "Truth" to be My Truth, and no one else's. I've found "Love" to be the pure, unconditional love of the universe. And I now know that "God and Love and Truth" are all One and the same.

I invite you to find the words that work for you. I hope you can hear my words and know that they are mine. You must find your own. I talk of the Divine, and this is God to me. Please know that I have no judgment or thoughts as to who you are writing to or connecting with. I just know that we are all Divine, no matter what we call Him/Her/It. The following is an example of one of my journals entries.

*Journals with God; Canvas #18 10/25/03:*

This writing and conversation started with me writing my prayers to God. I knew that when you started to write back to me – it was you because of how it felt. I call you God, and you sign as God, but who are you really?

*Hmmm, big question. Everything. I could stop but I know you are trying to put some context to this experience. I am the one energy of the Universe to the billionth infinity power... I am the God of every religion and name, yet I am not my name. I am indescribable, yet recognizable in everything. I talk to you as I do everyone who cares to listen – or not. I am the truth in your heart and the love in your soul. I also live in your pain and sadness. I am experience and choice. And everything is perfect. You are a part of me that I recognize as all of me. It's like the drop and the ocean. You are as great as the ocean, even though you only know yourself as the drop. So I tell you again – everything is just one thing: Me.*

*Love,*
*God*

# Introduction

There is something that once you know it... changes everything. That something is who you truly are.

Many people are searching for a sense of place and peace with who they are or are wondering what they should be doing in this life. This book will teach you practical techniques for connecting to the source of your soul. These techniques will not only help you to connect but also give you access to the truth of who you are and discover what you truly want to do in this life.

**Here is an invitation.**
**An invitation to know who you truly are.**

From my *Journals with God* I write to all:

*Greetings my Dear One: I am so pleased to be able to invite you to the truth of your Soul. I am here and want to talk with you every day. There is a path you can take to become your Soul, and that is through the practice of conversing with your Soul. Your mind has learned and believes that it is separate from the divinity that you are. You can break this belief and experience true connection and oneness through direct access and communion with the wisdom and divine knowledge that you possess. You can learn from yourself. There are many paths to this knowledge, but journaling and writing are a way that you can capture the messages and words so they become concrete and real. Everyone has the wisdom of the divine within them. Everyone can access it. This is a gift that you can give yourself. Make the commitment, make the time, make the effort.*

*Become One with Me.*

*Love,*
*God*

# Journey to the Soul

In July of 2002 I had come to a point in my life where I hit a wall. I realized that I could no longer go on with my life like it was and I would either need to kill myself or figure out why I was not happy. I had been depressed on and off all of my life. Despite doing what I thought I was supposed to be doing; having good jobs, several relationships and doing lots of fun and exciting things, I felt disconnected to everything and everyone. Something was missing. Before I understood what I was doing, I quit my job and set out on a spiritual journey to "find myself".

I began writing my prayers in my journal and after a while, I started hearing a voice that was giving me answers. I started to write down what I was hearing – which was being signed by God. God was writing to me – in response to my questions and pleadings. At first, I did not believe it. I was totally confounded by what was appearing on the pages. I found myself arguing, fighting, and even yelling at God! But whoever was responding to me was telling me what I now know is the truth. These were the most loving, caring, and insightful things anyone has ever told me. In the times when I was the most despondent, I would get true, caring responses like this one:

God, what do you want me to do!?

*Nothing, Diane.*

(Now I'm feeling disappointed and incredulous and in my head saying – yeah, right.)

*Yes, that is the message. You don't HAVE to DO anything. You can sit under a tree for the rest of your life. Your depression comes from your belief that you have to do something. Well you don't. Focus on fun, joy and love. From there, your joyous action is my love in motion!*

*Love,*
*God*

- From the *Journals with God (Pink book)* – *Dec. 11, 2002*

This was confounding to me because what I was writing felt so true. I certainly could not be writing from God, because, well, God would not be writing to me! But after many months of this type of writing I picked up a book called *"Conversations with God, Book 1"* by Neale Donald Walsch. I started reading it and felt that I had heard many of the concepts before – but what I realized was I had written many of the concepts before. Here was confirmation. Here was God speaking to someone else – the same messages! I might actually be writing to God and God might actually be writing to me!

As I read several of the books by Neil Donald Walsch and others, I found myself putting down on paper what I would be reading the next day. The phenomenon of picking up a book and reading a passage that applied very appropriately was happening to me over and over again. I was being led – no, pushed – to a new level of understanding that stretched the boundaries of my beliefs. What I was mainly being asked to do was look at the TRUTH. My Truth. *"In every moment of every day, what is the Truth"*? Still struggling with even wanting to be here (as in alive), I did not want to go back to my old life or have any part of it. But I knew that if I did not go to work soon, I would need to sell my house. I decided that finding this "Truth" for myself was the most important thing I could do, no matter what the consequences.

My journaling experience became more intense and more pointed. I was expressing on paper what was happening with me and God was responding through my hand. Still in the depths of depression, I had a glimmer of hope. I was beginning to understand that I might just be here for a reason. What kept me going were my journals and my connection with the One who was communicating with me.

Now I have been told that I would teach this through my actions, words and life. I was asked by God several times: "What would you do if you knew you were God?" It took me over a year to accept that I am God. Now living from this knowing and learning, I want to share this gift. My hope is that you find it a valuable part of your path in your Journey to the Soul.

# Honesty and the Truth

Excruciating, complete honesty, I realized, was the first step. Your journaling is a very personal, private experience, which you can choose to share or keep to yourself. But you must be willing to hear whatever is written, no matter what it is. It is this willingness that will tear down the walls that you have built which keep you from knowing and feeling and being "who you truly are".

In my journals God admonished me to ... *stop lying to each other and yourselves. And stop believing the lies – especially the ones you tell....*

From the *Journals with God, Canvas # 62*

Learning the truth about yourself requires rigorous self-honesty, the practice of which must go beyond you. Once the commitment to being honest is made, the realization soon follows that you must be honest with everyone around you. Most people think of themselves as honest, and I believe that there are varying degrees of "socially accepted honesty". Society, the media, business, laws, religions, have all created a set of rules that constitute polite honesty or the ideas of right and wrong based on doctrine and laws, which has skewed our understanding of the truth. The truth is not what causes the least pain for others; the truth must be what causes the least pain for ourselves, or more accurately, what honors ourselves. In so doing, the Divine is honored, which honors everyone. It is essential to become very clear about where you find your real truth. The only place you can discover this is from your own heart, your "gut" – your soul.

This is what God has again written to me: ...

*Ask yourself again and again: What is the Truth? Then tell it with all of your being.*

*Love,*
*God*

# Daily Practice

Practice is the way we become proficient at something or learn something new. A practice is a term used for spiritual rituals and activities that we repeat on a regular basis. The way to open a spiritual connection is through dedicated practice. I will offer you several ideas to use to create your own.

Many people have found that a lifetime of spiritual connection comes from a lifetime of spiritual practice. The connection comes easier over time and becomes part of who you are. You may be connected without the practice, but the connection is strengthened through the practice. The practice may transform over time, but it is a dedication to spiritual connection that provides the desire to continue to do the practice.

You may also find that your connection is showing up through visions, imagery, pictures or dreams. Then draw pictures or describe your images; write down your dreams. Everyone is different, and this process may be the catalyst for you to truly find your own process and practice. Nothing is wrong. Take this concept and make it your own.

My spiritual practice is my lifeline. I write at least once a day and sometimes more. I have my notebook, canvases, laptop, audio recorder, guitar – everything I need to capture whatever I feel is coming through me – around me whenever I'm home. I have my notebook and recorder with me if I'm working away from home and have found myself writing during breaks or riding in a car to a trade show. When I'm on a defined schedule, I write before work and at night before bed. I like the mornings and I like to get up, get ready for work or my day, then sit down with a spiritual book and read for a few minutes. I always have at least one spiritual book in progress. I find that this gets my mind on the right track.

This journaling process is about connection, but it is also about teaching the mind new truths. After reading a chapter or so, I will then go into meditation. I spend at least 10 minutes – sometimes up to 2 hours (when I feel I need it and have the time) focusing on feeling the Divine within me. Then I write for 10 to 30 minutes or hours. (I must admit to being late for work more than a few times during very intense periods when a lot was being written, but it was worth it.)

## Sacred Time – Sacred Space

I think one of the most important parts of this practice is creating sacred time and sacred space. I like to go to Sunday Services at Sunrise Ranch, the home of the Emissaries of Divine Light. They have a beautiful sanctuary, always set up with candles, music, flowers or decorations. This is a beautiful way to share and receive sacred time and space.

But I realize I need this sacred time and space myself every day, so I have created it very simply in my home. My art studio has a very comfortable couch I like to settle into. This is sacred space for me.

On the table in front of the couch I have a Peruvian offering blanket, an eagle fetish, and some candles. Many people create altars with objects that remind them of what is sacred. Sometimes I play soothing music. Lighting the candles sets the tone and also sets my intention. It reminds me that it is not the time to make the phone call I just remembered or deal with the laundry. It is the time that has been set aside to focus on my connection to all things – so I can go to my world from the best place I can.

# Spiritual Reading

There are probably thousands of books available on conscious awareness and spiritual awakening. I like the authors: don Miguel Ruiz, Eckhart Tolle, Neale Donald Walsch, Oriah Mountain Dreamer, Gandhi, Tolstoy, Paramahansa Yogananda, Sue Frederick and many others. I also enjoy reading works on Buddhism, Christianity, Judaism, the Emissaries of Divine Light and many other spiritual traditions.

I have found I am now seeing deeper and deeper levels of truth in all the traditions when the concept of separation is removed. We are all One and part of everything and we all can have access to the wisdom and Love of the One. When you remove all the "stories" in the traditional texts, you see the underlying message of our Oneness. Reading other work is the mirror for me. I find great richness and support for what I am discovering about myself. It is how we learn from each other.

For the examples, I am including some of my writing from the *Journals with God; the Canvas Journals*. In August of 2003, after about 1000 hand written pages, I became compelled to start doing this writing on 4' by 4' canvases. I would not know what I would write until each day, journaling with paint directly on canvas.

At first I was terrified to do this so the first canvas I wrote said:

*"Don't care what anyone thinks about you; remember who you are."*

# Meditation

There are many books and practices on meditation, so I will not go into detail here. You are welcome to use whatever works for you. For me, meditation is about simply closing my eyes, relaxing my body and focusing my thoughts – either for a specific intention or to quiet them down. I will offer some suggestions for these exercises and concepts like the following:

As you start your meditation, move into stillness. Watch your feelings and thoughts. As you notice your thoughts, watch them like watching yourself watch a movie. Thoughts will come, but your practice of watching the thoughts and watching the thinker will allow you to separate yourself from your identity with your mind. Gently let those thoughts go by – for just a moment. Focus on the thought of the Divine coming to talk with you. Focus on a vision of sitting in the presence of God and feeling the peace that is there.

Here I would like you to consider the idea that you have an awareness that is separate from your mind. With this awareness you will start to realize that even though you are not your mind, it is still a part of you, and you still have beliefs, attitudes and judgments. What you are about to do is to delve into the truth of who you truly are. You are looking to see where your beliefs, attitudes and judgments are causing you harm, and are really not from your truth. This is a journey into the truth, where the truth of your soul will be revealed, and it may bring you to places you are afraid to go.

# Journaling

On a practical note, I believe it is good to use a journal that is easy to write in and large. I like to use an unlined 9" x 11" sketchbook for my journals – when I'm not painting on canvas. They allow me freedom with lots of space and pages. Use what works for you. I do suggest that you try writing through your hands, but if you feel like you are ultimately drawn to type on a keyboard, please follow that impulse.

My process begins by writing the date and location. I then start writing as if I am writing a prayer or a letter to my best friend, and want to express what is going on with me. I rant and rage and let it out. I am now talking to the Divine. I call the Divine "God", which is the name I know for the One Energy of the Universe.

You may write to whomever you know as this Divine one for you. This is your time to be with the Divine. This is your time to say whatever you want about what is going on in your life. This is the time to begin your conversation with God. Write with an open heart and allow the feelings to fill you. As you are writing, ask yourself what the real burning question is right now that you want to know the truth about. Begin this with the attitude of knowing that you can hear and receive the wisdom and guidance from the Divine through your mind, hands, heart and pen.

As God has written to me:

*I talk to you as I do everyone who cares to listen – or not.*

*Journals with God, Canvas #16 10/24/03*

When I felt like I had gotten it out, I would ask what I felt was the most honest question I had about what was going on. Then I would write my name..."Diane"...and listen for the words...

*...thank you for writing this. This is a very good thing you are doing right now for people who want to know how to connect with Me. This is going to be very helpful. This is an excellent start in sharing your work with others – and sharing the real message which is; everyone can do this. I am so excited about how many people we will touch. All for now...*

*Love,*
*God*

Just as in this example, I would listen for a word, then write it - repeating this process. I would "hear" words and as I was writing more I started expecting certain answers. I had to get my mind out of the way and listen with my heart. From the surrendered heart you will receive the words of God.

The amazing thing was, I never got what I (my ego) expected. A few people who have read some of my Journals with God on canvas have commented that, "you really didn't get your question answered". But the truth is, God had answered the real question in my heart on a higher level than the concepts of the earthly plain, at a point where She was stretching my comprehension. All of this was stretching my comprehension. I did not believe that I am God. I have heard that God is within us, but not that She is us. I could not grasp that. But after hundreds of pages of her telling me that She and I are One and that I could know the thoughts of God, I started getting it. This was discovering who I truly am (who we all are). Knowing this by experiencing this through feeling the connection every day and hearing the words of God become mine.

The message from God would always be perfect, concise and always loving; sometimes lovingly blunt. I needed the proverbial 2 x 4 across the head and God would wake me up over and over again to increasingly higher levels of understanding. She also would know exactly what I was ready to hear, even when I didn't get it right away.

Occasionally I would go back and read something I wrote days before thinking "I don't get this". I would then "get it", like a ton of bricks just fell on me. I prayed to know the truth, and I got it, in spades. But as Christ has said, "Pray for anything, you have it, it's yours". I have said and always seem to experience: be careful what you ask for, because you always get it.

So, the question I have for you is, "Are you ready?" Are you really ready to learn who you truly are and to live as that person? Are you ready to walk into the pain of the delusion that you have been living and be willing to face it? Are you ready to hear what lies you and others you've trusted have been telling you for years? Are you ready to listen to the truth? This is the commitment that you must make in order to walk this path.

So, with that, if you believe that you, too, can hear from God, you will. I am telling you that you can; God has said that everyone can, so now it is up to you. Are you ready to start?

# Prayer

Today I have come to the silent stillness with a desire to know. Oh Divine One, who is the Truth of me, please speak to me with your love, wisdom and compassion. Please let me know what I need to know today to further me on my journey to becoming One with You.

# Examples

Here are 10 different examples I have used and have heard of others using to approach opening up to Divine connection. I suggest that you read through the entire book. When you do your daily practice, choose the example that fits that day's situation, or create your own. Use the same one every day if you want, or try different ones, exploring the options. The purpose of this book is to help you create your practice for your Journey to the Soul.

## *Practice Example 1*

## Writing with a Friend

Take a few breaths to relax. Then read the following meditation and close your eyes. Breathe deeply and relax your body, feeling the presence of the Divine. Meditate for at least 5 minutes and up to 20 minutes using the above techniques. Begin to write as though you are writing to your best friend for advice. Tell Him/Her what is going on in your life and ask for their advice. Now, really feel this as a prayer and recognize that your best friend truly is the Divine One within you. When you are done with the question, write your name as if you were reading their response....and listen. Write what you hear. Whatever it is. Just listen for the words. Don't judge it, but patiently expect to hear – because you *can* hear. Open your heart and your mind and trust that you will hear. If not today, perhaps tomorrow or the next day. If you need to, just imagine what you best friend would say to you. This can help you open the door to the deeper truth to come through. Believe that you can year the Divine and with patience you will remove the walls you've created to keep yourself from hearing the truth. You know who you are, and you know that you can know this One.

## Reading

*Journals with God, Canvas # 21 10/28/03*

God, I feel like I'm asking the same questions but it seems to be hard to 'be my soul'. How do we do this?

*My Love, you are this. All you need to do is remember this. I know it is not easy, as that is the way this life has been designed. As I said, it starts with a commitment to yourself (Me) and a desire from your heart to know your soul. This is a prayer and it will be answered. The answers will come as the truth of your heart and will bring feelings of love, joy, peace and contentment. But, you need to make room and time for this prayer. You must face your mind and your beliefs that you are anything but this. There is nothing outside you that can show you who you are. You must some how, some way, go within. Take the power of this prayer and confront every fear and negative feeling and ask to know the truth. Know that I am right here and as scary as this may seem, know that nothing can touch you.*

*Love,*
*God*

**Close your eyes and begin...**

## *Practice Example 2*

## Feeling Disconnected

There are times where we feel very far from being connected. This is where our practice can be especially helpful. Take a few breaths to relax, then read the following meditation. Close your eyes and meditate for 5 to 10 minutes. If you feel your mind taking over and not giving you peace, then just start writing – no format, no rules, just let your thoughts and ideas flow. Write for at least 3 pages and even if you think you don't have anything else to write, keep writing. Even if it does not seem important, write whatever is coming to mind. Keep writing as many pages as possible. Just let it out and see where it goes. This is lowering your defenses and allowing Spirit to flow. This is getting your mind through with its thoughts, attitudes and judgments, and moving into the expression of the Soul.

## Reading

*Journals with God, Canvas # 23 11/02/03*

God, today I'm feeling a bit down and disconnected. I don't really feel like writing, but here I am...

*So, My Love, did you forget that you are also human? Of course you are feeling "out of it" (Your favorite term for this feeling). You went to a concert and stayed up half the night, and now your body is feeling it. You are also being affected by your body's monthly cycle, which roots you very energetically with the creative forces of the earth. That is why this time feels very powerful and sometimes overwhelming. Keep doing what you are doing and be loving and patient with yourself. In these times you also get caught up in panicking over everything you feel you have to do, to the point of doing nothing. But today, you started here with me, so you are connected. And with this connection you can keep doing what you want even when you are feeling down. You know you can always find Me here and you know you can also feel Me here. You are filled with All My Love.*

*Love,*
*God*

**Close your eyes and begin....**

# *Practice Example 3*

## The Truth

This is a meditation about surrendering to the truth, which is the core of this work. It's about relationships, major decisions, family, friends, work, money, home-life, kids, etc. This is the place where regular mind solutions aren't cutting it. This is going to the Soul. As you write, use the question format and ask with great surrender and willingness to hear the truth, no matter what it is. Many times, what will be written will not even address what you think the question is. Let it and follow it wherever it leads you. Trust the Writer.

## Reading

*Journals with God, Canvas # 4 10/01/03*

God, what is this truth? How do I find this "Truth"? This seems so hard.

*My Love, go to peace. And in every moment of every day, ask yourself: is what you are doing, saying, and being, from the truth of your heart? You can't ask your soul this question and not get an honest answer. Now, you have a choice: listen and follow this truth – and live in the peace and love of your heart, or live in delusion and fear. For not living in what is true for you is living in delusion. You know this – as you have felt like "a stranger in your own skin." Ask the question. I will answer.*

*Love,*
*God*

**Close your eyes and begin....**

# *Practice Example 4*

## Forgiveness

This meditation and writing is dealing with resistance, forgiveness and acceptance. Many times we want to find the peace in our hearts, but still feel pain somewhere. Much of the path to finding the truth is in accepting what is. Much of our own pain is in resisting what is or holding negative energy around things that have happened. The way through this and finding peace is through forgiveness. If you are feeling anger, hurt, pain, resentment, sadness, or betrayal toward someone else, a situation, or even yourself, you can do forgiveness work around it. This writing is some the most powerful work you can do.

The process is done by starting a dialog with the person, situation, or the part of you that is holding the resistance. First start with laying out what happened: all the attitudes, judgments; what was hurtful, painful and why. Then respond as the other person or part of you would respond if you were actually talking with them. Next, change your perspective. Now allow and be the Divine One within you and explain what happened again from the place of everyone having done their best. You can write here that you do not condone or will not allow this to happen again, but that you are willing to release the anger and pain as well as the energy of resistance to what happened. Write what you need to in order to respect yourself and care for yourself, knowing that releasing this pain and anger is the greatest thing you can do to free yourself to find peace. Write and say "I forgive you". And so it will be.

Read the following and begin your meditation with a prayer asking the Divine to be with you at this very difficult time. Pray to be protected and guided and to feel the love of the Presence.

## Reading

*Journals with God, Canvas # 75 11/10/04*

## Forgiveness

*My Love, my prayer for you is to know the love that is experienced in complete acceptance. You must accept everyone and everything exactly like it is. First you must accept your attitudes and judgments to recognize your non-acceptance – and then begin by forgiving yourself. As you forget who you are, you will fall back into delusion and not see the perfection in everything. Wake up My Love, and find your freedom in forgiveness.*

*Love,*
*God*

**Close your eyes and begin**....

## *Practice Example 5*

## Finding Peace

Connecting within. Finding peace. This is a time of focus and being in peace. Here the meditation is more important than the writing, but I would like you to have your journal next to you. Read the following and go into meditation. Truly have the intention of feeling the peace that is within you and the peace that you are. At the end of your meditation, ask the Divine one if there is anything He/She would like to tell you today... and write what you hear.

## Below are two readings:

*Journals with God, Canvas #71, 9/16/04*

*"If it is peace that you desire*
*Then come to peace. Trust is the way.*
*Truth is your gift to give.*
*For in your truth lives love.*
*In love lives your connection to everything.*
*In remembering who you are, you will find Me.*
*And this is the peace that passeth all understanding.*

*Love,*
*God*

*Journals with God, Canvas #31 11/13/03*

*Today you have come to the Silent Stillness without need or desire. There is no question to be answered or fear to be*

27

overcome. All there is is the peace of this moment. Feel the love that is here and the love that you are. Hear the words that are spoken from the depths of your soul and know it is I speaking to you. Remove the walls you have built around your heart to protect yourself. They have only served to keep your love from getting out. From this place of stillness, touch the love in your heart and feel the power within you. This is your connection to everything and everyone. And from this place you remember who you are. So now I ask you:

What would you do if you knew you were God?

Love,
God

**Close your eyes and begin....**

## *Practice Example 6*

## Divine Creation

This is what I call "meditation creation". When you are feeling good and not dealing with an issue at hand or block to be overcome, you can use this to help propel you in creating. Sometimes there might be something you are trying to create or a problem you want to solve. In this practice, write about the problem or question for a few minutes then go into meditation and then release it. Watch what thoughts come. Start writing what you hear.

## Reading

*Journals with God, Canvas #10 10/15/04*

Ok, God, I must be crazy! I'm painting, writing songs, thinking of a hundred canvases with You – and oh yeah, I'm almost out of money. On top of this, who's going to believe that You are really writing to ME!?

*Who cares? This is what living in your truth is about. You have hundreds of pages of our conversations, so you know what is true for you. Now that you are becoming one who remembers, your joy has made you want to share this. You felt that this writing was too big to just copy on to small print. And this direct experience of Me writing through you is part of what you want to share. I am overjoyed that you want to share Me and our love with everyone! Keep dreaming "crazy dreams." The example of you living your life in truth, trust and love will teach more than a thousand canvases. But please don't stop writing, as this is part of living your truth. I love it too!*

*Love,*
*God*

**Close your eyes and begin...**

## *Practice Example 7*

## Anything Goes

Here you can bring out your canvas and paints, paper and pens, pastels, or markers. This is opening yourself up to create in a larger format and face any fears around your expression. This is where you can allow yourself to create, write, move and respond from a pure place of the Divine.

Read the following canvas, then go to a quiet mind meditation. Ask the Divine to work through you and allow whatever comes. Release the need to see the image or words on the paper or canvas before you move. Start the impulse by reaching toward the pens or brush and let the impulse pull you through. If you want to try something farther outside your comfort zone, use your left hand (or right if you are left-handed),. Follow the impulses and let whatever is created come. There is so much creativity in your heart, allowing it to flow will open space for more.

## Reading

*Journals with God, Canvas #9 10/14/03*

God, in the past 24 hours, I spent most of my time quiet and alone. I am feeling at peace. I am feeling your Love. And I know that this writing and my painting is the highest expression of my Truth right now. In trust and love and joy I allow myself to create with abandon. God, with You I am ready to fly!

*My Love, you are flying! What a metaphor. By dropping fear and thoughts of limitation, you truly do allow your spirit to soar. You are seeing your dreams expand and grow by the minute. All is possible! Keep trusting. Keep loving. And you will live in the greatest joy you have ever experienced. For this is My joy!*

*Love,*
*God*

**Close your eyes and begin....**

# *Practice Example 8*

## Sacred Workout

I feel my best when I am taking care of my mind, body and spirit. And with the reality of this world, sacred time is sometimes difficult to find or create. One of the things I have recognized is that my very important physical exercise or "workout" has become sacred time. I like to walk, run, bike or hike. I love getting into nature and will make this time a moving meditation. Sometimes I will listen to a spiritual book on tape, meditative or worship music but what I enjoy most is silence or the sound of the wind. I open my awareness to the aliveness of the plants, trees and rocks around me and under my feet, remembering my connection to them. I then focus my mind on being very much in this moment – what I see and the feeling of my body moving, with grace and strength.

I will sometimes think of an issue or problem I am trying to solve at the beginning of my workout and then make a conscious decision to set it aside, to let it rest. I can't tell you how many times I would have a new solution or idea pop into my head while I was out on my bike or running along a trail. I love it when it happens. I get excited and can't wait to get home to write it down. This is where audio recorders could be handy if you find this happens to you a lot.

When possible, I will go home and take some time to slow down, meditate for a few minutes and then write for as long as I can. These times can by very clear and creative as a lot of stress has been released and energy is moving. If I do not have much time, I would at least write down any ideas that came up during the workout.

This reading is inspiration to keep doing your practice, even when times are good.

## Reading

*Journals with God, Canvas #32 11/10/03*

God, I've moved from a perpetual feeling of wanting to know what I should be doing to feeling at peace with what I have chosen to do right now. But what I now understand is it is not what I am doing that has brought me peace, but my connection to the true desires of my soul. From here what I do is the expression of that Truth and that is what brings me joy. This is what You have been telling me. I feel like I am just now beginning to live. Thank You for this love and peace.

*My Love, you are learning – not from what I have been telling you, but from your experience. These subtle shifts in awareness have come from your faith and your commitment to that faith. From a place of not knowing you trusted your heart to tell you the truth. And you waited. For through your battles with the old beliefs of your mind, you stayed true to your faith. And your commitment to only living from the truth of your soul has brought you this new perspective. Everything starts from you being the truth and love of your soul. You now know this as you are this. And you are now experiencing the truth of this, and you teach this by sharing your experience and by being the truth and love that you are. This is all there is to do.*

*Now get on your shoes and move!*

*Love,*
*God*

## *Practice Example 9*

## Song and Dance

I have written many songs since I started doing this practice. I feel the flow of expression coming through in many, many ways: painting, writing, jewelry, symbols; and now music and songs. But the most beautiful expression is how I am with others. I am authentically myself. In many of the pages God had written the question to me: "What would you do if you knew you were God?" The answer has come: live from the Divine impulse. Express, create, be and do what my heart feels compelled to do. This is living as the Divine. This is living in Love.

Sing, play an instrument, dance, drum....allow authentic expression to flow. Go into a meditative space with your instruments, movements, voice, or all three.

One day while playing my guitar I started strumming a new tune and singing the following words. The entire piece came through in just two days:

*What would you do if you knew you were God?*
by Diane Dandeneau © 2004-2016

*What would you do if you knew you were God?*
*Who would you be if you knew you were God?*
*How would you feel about the world if you knew*
*That everything is all God too? ...*

*What would the truth be if there were no fear?*
*Would you allow wars, famine or tears?*
*How would you touch the world with your love*
*If you knew that that's all there was?*

*Hmmmmmmm, Hmmmmmmm*

*The dance with the darkness allures and appears*
*To be the way of the world and its fears*
*But when you shine the light on the truth*
*You see that it's all just a ruse.*

*There'll be a time when you'll tire of the pain*
*When you will ask, what's the point of this game?*
*But when you look at the truth behind all*
*You realize that we choose it all.*

*Hmmmmmmm, Hmmmmmmm*

*With hands made of fire and minds made of steel*
*Do we choose to build weapons, do we choose to heal?*
*When you live from the love in your heart*
*The answer to that's not so hard...*

*What would you do if you knew you were God?*
*Who would you be if you knew you were God?*
*What would you do if you knew that you have -*
*The power of creation right –*
*Right in your hands*
*Right in your hands*
*Right in your hands*
*Right in your hands*

*What would you do if you knew you were God?*

**Close your eyes and begin....**

## *Practice Example 10*

## Connecting to Who You Are and Banishing Fear

This last exercise is a reminder as to what this whole exercise is about – connecting to the truth of who you are and living from that place. We need to do this work because we are not always living as our true selves. What keeps us from who we are is our fear, learned from a lifetime of living in the world of fear. This process is what we can use to identify our fears and see how we keep ourselves from feeling the love, joy and peace of being who we are. This requires trusting the Divine and listening.

In your meditation, look within for any feeling of anxiety, nervousness, uneasiness, anger, disappointment, etc. Notice your energy and feel. It is important to acknowledge those feelings, but it also important to know that they are there to show us our false beliefs, to show us where we are not dealing with something or being honest with ourselves. These feelings are telling us the truth about what we think. But the biggest thing we must do is to see what is coming from fear and that we don't have to be afraid. Face your fears then ask who they are, why they are there, and what they can teach you. Then ask yourself if they are telling you the truth or not. This may require some forgiveness work after you discover the real root of the feelings. In my experience, when I have written about what I was afraid of, the power in it dissipated. I could see very clearly the delusions I believed and was able to see them for what they really are. This is the power of this process. This is a true door to freedom, and it is a door you can open for yourself.

# Reading

*Journals with God, Canvas #6 10/10/04*

God, I do trust you. And I am even beginning to remember that I am You. But I have to live in this world and this world is run by fear. It seems impossible to find the truth when just about everyone believes in fear.

*My Love, the world has forgotten that we are body, mind, and spirit. The body and mind are how you experience life, but your spirit – your connection to Me – is who you are. When you believe in the world created by the mind and forget who you are, you will be afraid. In your current society you do not teach of infinite love and oneness. You teach that you are what you know and what you have done. You teach that happiness is found outside yourself and that I am far away. Your heart knows the truth and is crying out. It is time to listen to the truth of your heart and recognize the mind as the one that has learned from the fears of an unconscious society and believes that is the truth. You are teaching your mind a new truth. One that comes from a greater depth of knowing than you have ever experienced:*

*YOU ARE GOD AND GOD IS NOT AFRAID.*

*Love,*
*God*

**Close your eyes and begin....**

# Thank You

Thank you for your effort and hard work. As you do this practice, you will realize that all of life is sacred time and sacred space. I believe that the more people begin to wake up and connect with truth and Source the more love, joy and peace there will be in the world. And as God has written to me, *"there is no other way"*. I am doing my best to do my part. Thank you for doing your part.


With Love and Blessings

~ Diane Dandeneau

# About the Author

Living in the mountains of Colorado, Diane Dandeneau is an Artist, Author, Speaker, Singer-Songwriter, Teacher, Serial Entrepreneur, and Activist. She shares her experiences of spiritual connection to inspire others through her art, books, speaking, music, workshops and programs. With this work she is answering the question: "What would you do if you knew you were God?"

Diane Dandeneau Studios, LLC publishes and distributes the paintings, jewelry, music, books, audiobooks, and online programs by Diane Dandeneau and friends.

To learn more please visit the website at: www.dianedandeneau.com, or call the studio to receive a brochure.

*Journey to the Soul* is a companion to these upcoming books also by Diane Dandeneau:

### *The Year of Awakening*
### Journey to Living a Divinely Guided Life

### *The Art of Extraordinary Success*
### Living in the Zone of Creative Mastery

## Art

Her journey to the soul has taken her to places near and far to explore sacred sites from around the world and to paint her series – *In Search of the Sacred*.

You can see her work from the Southwest U.S., Mexico and Machu Picchu, Peru on her web site at: www.dandeneau.com.

## Music

In 2011 she produced her first music CD: What Would You Do if You Knew You Were God? This is available at: www.dianedandeneau.com.

She also performs Keynote Concerts and special music for New Thought faith communities and more progressive organizations and businesses.

## Journey to the Soul – 30-Day Journaling Challenge

If you would like to take this journey even deeper, you can take the online, Journey to the Soul, 30-Day Journaling Challenge. It includes additional teachings that go deeper into the healing discussed in this book, plus daily audio meditations and excerpts from the Journey to the Soul Audiobook. This program will help you create your daily practice and cultivate your relationship with the Divine for truly living a Divinely Guided Life. Learn more at: www.journalswithgod.com.

## Speaking, Workshops and Coaching

Ms. Dandeneau is currently accepting bookings for speaking, workshops and keynote concerts. She works with people interested in integrating these principles into life and business. She brings her inspirational programs to New Thought spiritual communities and general audiences. Learn more at:

http://www.dianedandeneau.com/speakingworkshops/

# Unione Symbol

You may have noticed the swish with the circle on the cover and in the book after God's signature. As I was writing in my Journals with God, it just started showing up. One day I asked what it was:

10/25/03

Good morning God! Nice Saturday morning. I love the way you sign our journals. You say *"You and I are One"* when you write it. It is a beautiful symbol. Does it have a name?

*I told you, You and I are One.*

Well, that's kind of a long name.

*Spell it.*

(What I saw and wrote was:)

*U- N- I are One.*

*This is the symbol of the **union** of the human and Divine.*

*Love,*
*God*

I had goose bumps as I wrote this. I knew this was significant, but I didn't know how significant it was. And I knew it was true.

I wear this pendant and have made sterling silver pendants of this symbol that you too can wear to help you

remember that you too are One with the Divine.
www.uniareone.com

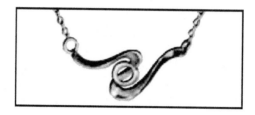

Thank you again for reading *Journey to the Soul.* I invite you to visit my blog to see the real canvas journals:

http://www.dianedandeneau.com/category/the_canvas_journals/

CPSIA information can be obtained
at www.ICGtesting.com
Printed in the USA
LVOW04s2131170316

479671LV00009B/21/P